A LOOK AT US HISTORY

THE TRANSCONTINENTAL RAILROAD

BY JOHN O'MARA

CRASHCOURSE

Please visit our website, www.garethstevens.com. For a free color catalog of all our high-quality books, call toll free 1-800-542-2595 or fax 1-877-542-2596.

Cataloging-in-Publication Data

Names: O'Mara, John.
Title: The Transcontinental Railroad / John O'Mara
Description: New York : Gareth Stevens Publishing, 2020. | Series: A look at U.S. history | Includes glossary and index.
Identifiers: ISBN 9781538248874 (pbk.) | ISBN 9781538248898 (library bound) | ISBN 9781538248881 (6 pack)
Subjects: LCSH: Pacific railroads--History--Juvenile literature. | Railroads--United States--History--Juvenile literature. | Frontier and pioneer life--United States--Juvenile literature.
Classification: LCC TF25.P23 O43 2020 | DDC 385.0973--dc23

First Edition

Published in 2020 by
Gareth Stevens Publishing
111 East 14th Street, Suite 349
New York, NY 10003

Editor: Therese M. Shea

Photo credits: Series art Christophe BOISSON/Shutterstock.com; (feather quill) Galushko Sergey/Shutterstock.com; (parchment) mollicart-design/Shutterstock.com; cover, p. 1 Archive Photos/Getty Images; p. 5 Everett Collection/Shutterstock.com; p. 7 George Skadding/The LIFE Picture Collection/Getty Images; p. 9 Carleton E. Watkins/wikimedia (https://commons.wikimedia.org/wiki/File:CPRR_Chief_Engineer_Theodore_D._Judah.jpg); p. 11 Courtesy of the Library of Congress; p. 13 City and County of San Francisco, California (bond); DigitalImageServices.com (scanning, reconstruction, digital restoration, and enhancement)/wikimedia (https://commons.wikimedia.org/wiki/File:San_Francisco_Pacific_Railroad_Bond_WPRR_1865.jpg); pp. 15, 29 Marzolino/Shutterstock.com; pp. 17, 23 Bettmann/Getty Images; p. 19 Historical/Corbis Historical/Getty Images; p. 21 PHAS/Universal Images Group/Getty Images; p. 25 Photoonlife/Shutterstock.com; p. 27 Andrew J. Russell/Wikimedia.

Printed in the United States of America

CPSIA compliance information: Batch #CW20GS: For further information contact Gareth Stevens, New York, New York at 1-800-542-2595.

CONTENTS

Words in the glossary appear in **bold** type the first time they are used in the text.

COAST TO COAST

For a long time, people had no easy way of traveling from one coast of the United States to the other. They could travel in wagons and **stagecoaches**. They could travel by ship too. Both ways of traveling were **difficult**, costly, and long.

MAKE THE GRADE

Some people traveling from one US coast to the other sailed around South America. Others sailed to Central America, took a train to the other side, and sailed up the coast.

TRAVELING BY RAIL

The building of the first US railroad began in 1828. Railroads made travel between large cities easier. Some people began planning to build a transcontinental railroad, or train tracks that crossed the whole country. It would be a hard job.

MAKE THE GRADE

The first steam **locomotive** built in America was called Tom Thumb. Coal-powered trains like this took the place of horse-drawn trains.

JUDAH'S PLAN

In 1860, **engineer** Theodore Judah planned a path for a transcontinental railroad through the Sierra Nevada mountains. He found **investors** for the railroad, and he got the US government to support the plan. However, Judah died before the transcontinental railroad was finished.

MAKE THE GRADE

The investors that Theodore Judah (above) found formed the Central Pacific Railroad Company.

THE PACIFIC RAILWAY ACT

In 1862, President Abraham Lincoln signed the Pacific Railway Act. It provided land and money for the building of a railroad across the country. The Central Pacific Railroad and the Union Pacific Railroad were the companies that would lay the tracks.

MAKE THE GRADE

The businessmen who controlled the Central Pacific were called the "Big Four." They were Leland Stanford, Charles Crocker, Collis P. Huntington, and Mark Hopkins.

ABRAHAM LINCOLN

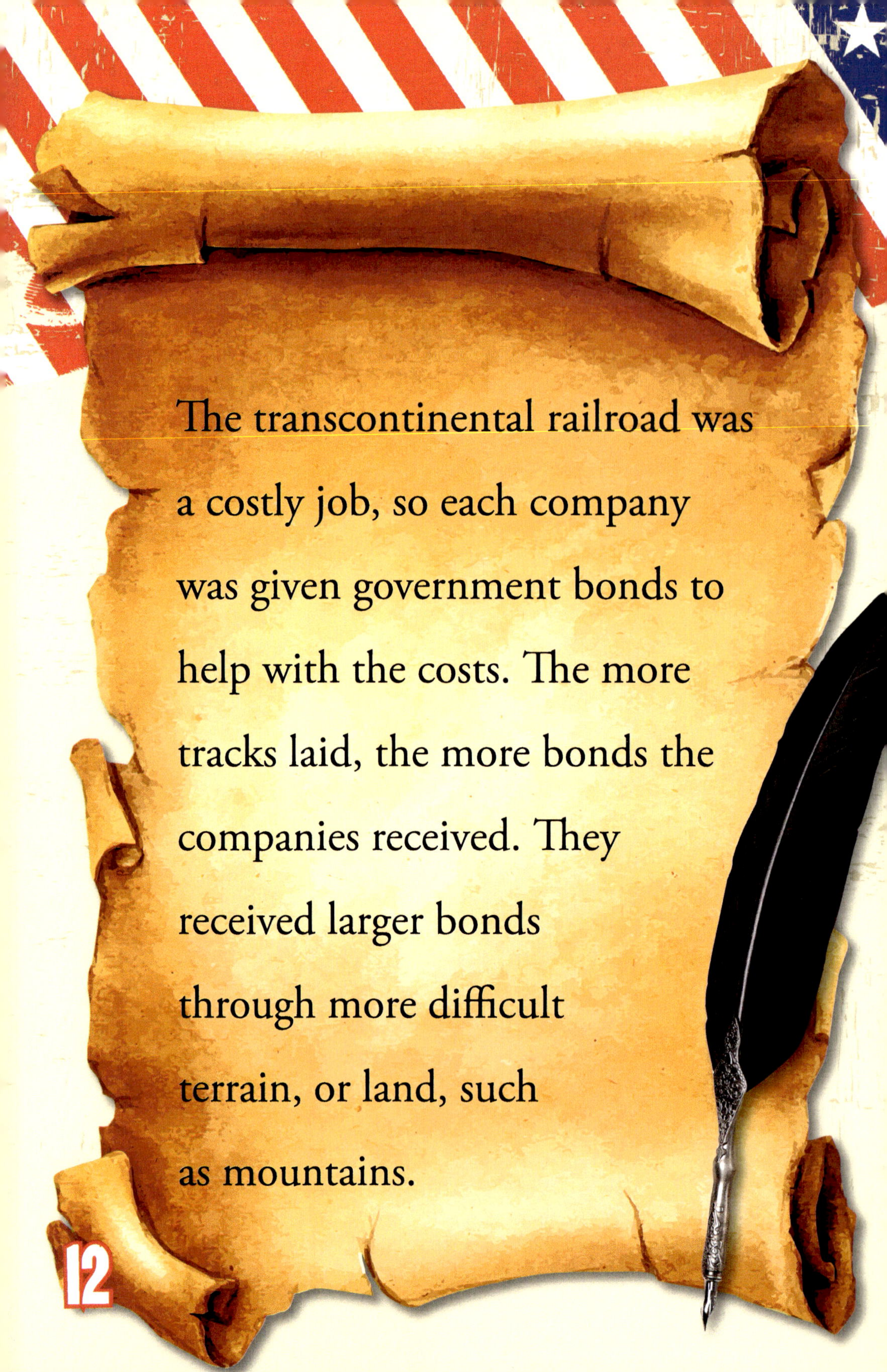

The transcontinental railroad was a costly job, so each company was given government bonds to help with the costs. The more tracks laid, the more bonds the companies received. They received larger bonds through more difficult terrain, or land, such as mountains.

MAKE THE GRADE

Bonds are a kind of loan that has to be paid back with more money, called interest.

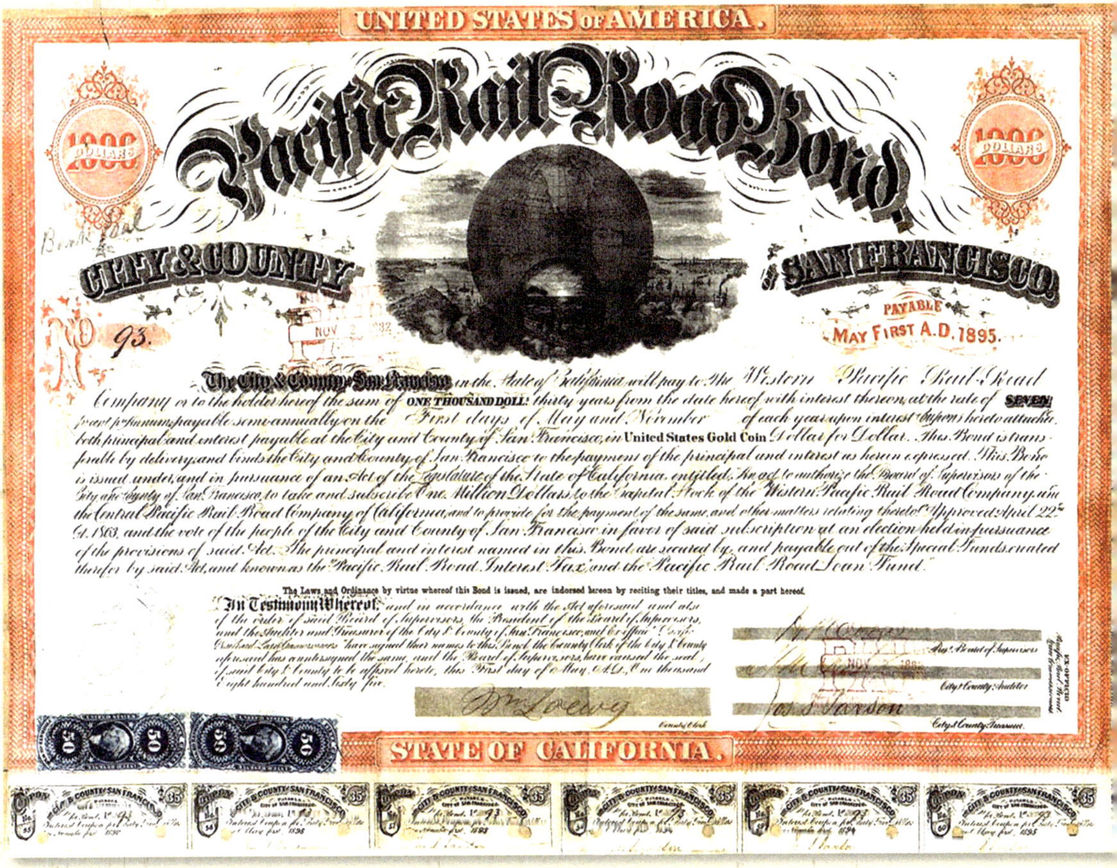

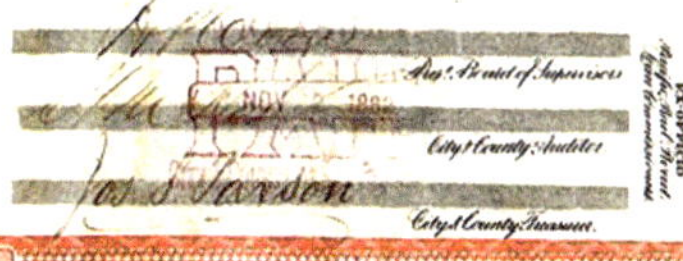

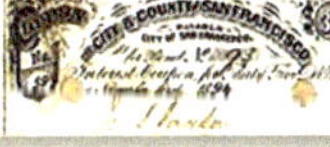

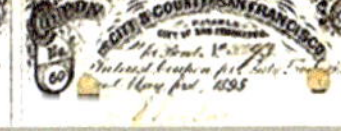

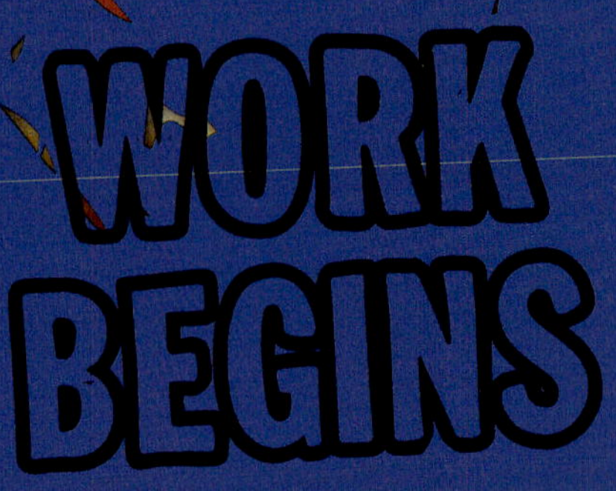

WORK BEGINS

In 1863, Central Pacific Railroad workers started in Sacramento, California, and laid track east. Union Pacific workers didn't start laying tracks until after the **American Civil War** ended in 1865. They built west from the border of Iowa and Nebraska.

MAKE THE GRADE

In 1864, the second Pacific Railway Act gave more land to the railroads. The railroads sold bonds and land to raise money for building.

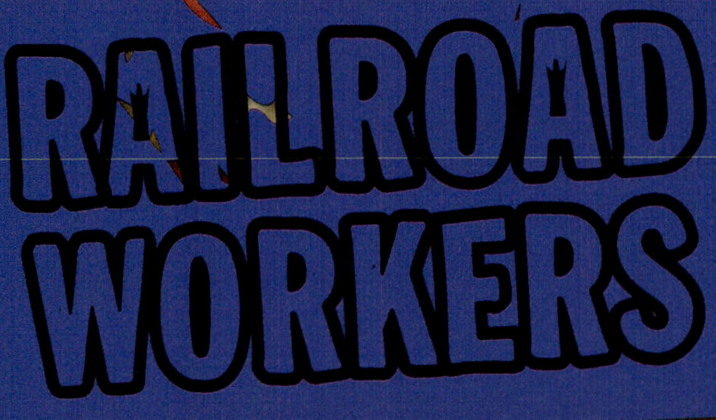

RAILROAD WORKERS

The railroads hired many kinds of people. Union Pacific hired Irish **immigrants** as well as men who had been Civil War soldiers. They also hired **Mormons** to lay tracks through Utah, where many Mormons settled. Work went quickly across the flat terrain.

MAKE THE GRADE

Union Pacific laid tracks across the lands of Native American peoples including the Sioux, Cheyenne, and Arapaho. Native Americans would then attack worker camps and ruin the tracks.

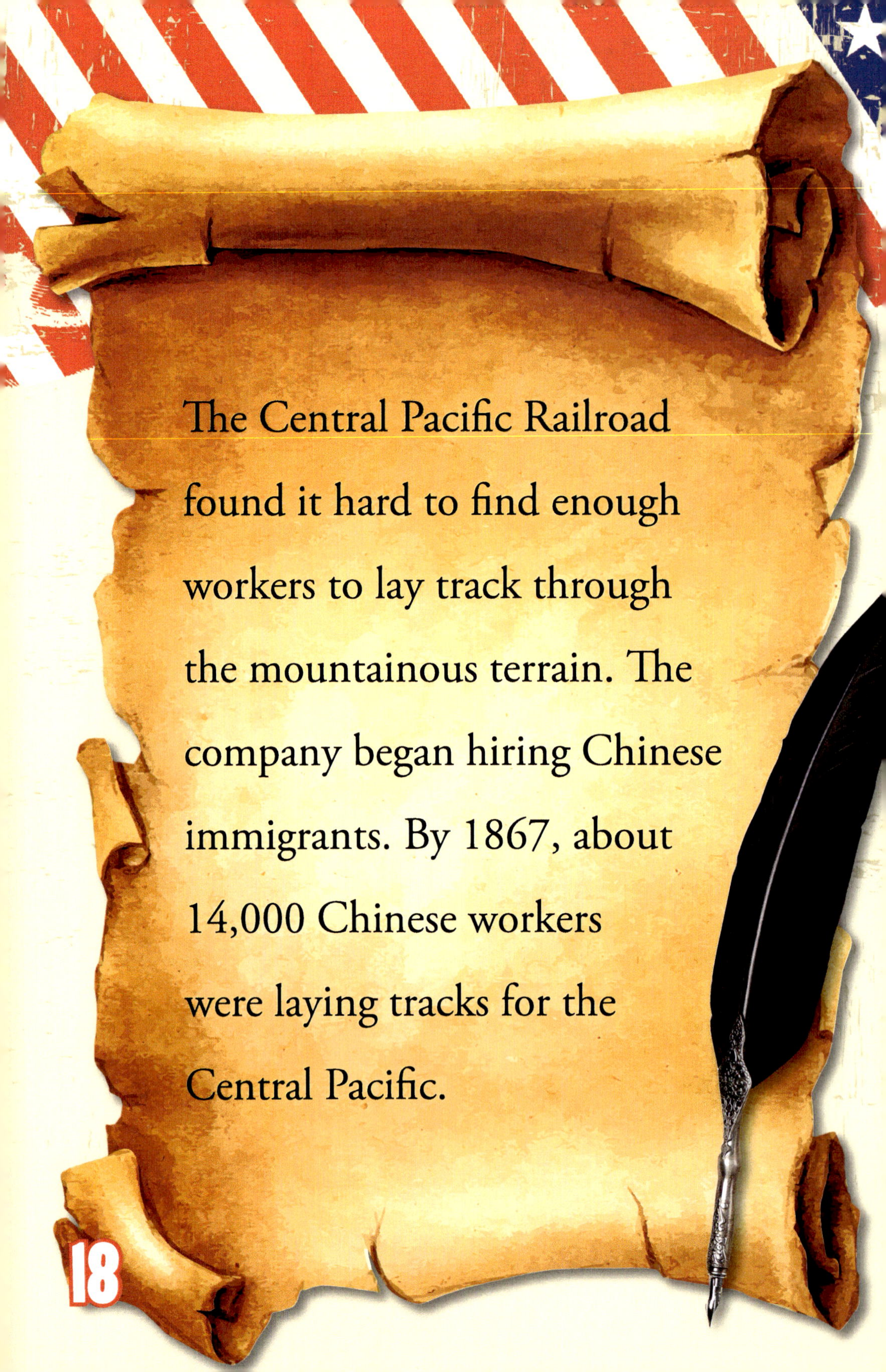

The Central Pacific Railroad found it hard to find enough workers to lay track through the mountainous terrain. The company began hiring Chinese immigrants. By 1867, about 14,000 Chinese workers were laying tracks for the Central Pacific.

MAKE THE GRADE

Chinese railroad workers were often treated unfairly. For example, they made less money than white workers.

DANGER!

Central Pacific railroad workers faced great dangers. They had to blast through mountains with **explosives.** They built high wooden bridges over valleys. Workers died of the cold and from **avalanches**, too. Hundreds died in the Sierra Nevada.

MAKE THE GRADE

Chinese workers stopped working for a time and asked for higher pay. Central Pacific wouldn't send food supplies to them until they went back to work.

A NEW RECORD

In early 1869, the Central Pacific and Union Pacific lines were close. They agreed to meet at Promontory Summit in Utah. In April, Central Pacific laid 10 miles (16 km) of track in a day, breaking the Union Pacific record by more than 2 miles (3.2 km).

MAKE THE GRADE

To complete their record, Central Pacific workers laid about 3,520 rails in a day. Each rail weighed around 560 pounds (254 kg).

THE LAST SPIKES

The tracks laid by Central Pacific and Union Pacific were finally joined at a **ceremony** at Promontory Summit on May 10, 1869. Central Pacific had laid about 690 miles (1,110 km) of track. Union Pacific had laid about 1,086 miles (1,748 km).

MAKE THE GRADE

Central Pacific had begun laying tracks earlier than Union Pacific. However, they completed fewer miles because of the mountainous terrain.

OR
ID
MT
ND
SD
WY
PROMONTORY SUMMIT
SACRAMENTO
OMAHA
NE
NV
UT
CO
CA
KS
AZ
NM
OK
TX

UNION PACIFIC RAILROAD

CENTRAL PACIFIC RAILROAD

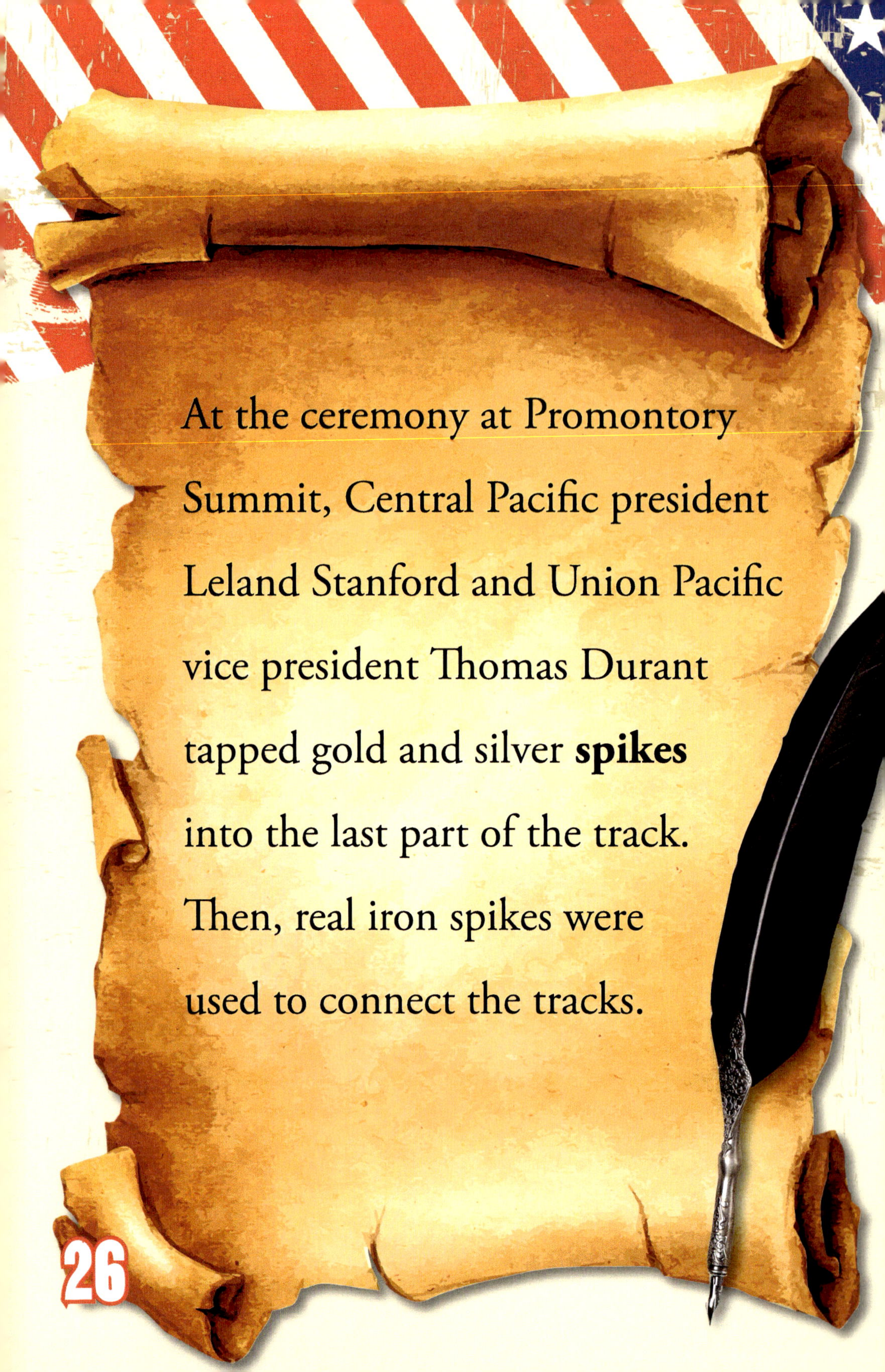

At the ceremony at Promontory Summit, Central Pacific president Leland Stanford and Union Pacific vice president Thomas Durant tapped gold and silver **spikes** into the last part of the track. Then, real iron spikes were used to connect the tracks.

MAKE THE GRADE

A **telegraph** line was connected to the railroad. When the last spike went in, a telegraph message was sent out that read: D-O-N-E.

RESULTS OF THE RAILROAD

After it was connected to eastern railroads, the new transcontinental railroad cut the time it took to cross the nation from about 6 months to less than 2 weeks. It was less costly too. The railroad changed the nation forever.

MAKE THE GRADE

The transcontinental railroad brought more people to native peoples' lands. Native settlements were destroyed, and Native Americans were forced to move.

KEY DATES OF THE TRANSCONTINENTAL RAILROAD

1860
Engineer Theodore Judah finds a path for a transcontinental railroad.

1861
The American Civil War begins.

1862
President Abraham Lincoln signs the Pacific Railway Act to support the building of the railroad.

1863
The Central Pacific Railroad starts laying track east in Sacramento, California.

1864
Lincoln signs another Pacific Railway Act that gives more land and larger government bonds to the railroad companies building the track.

1865
The American Civil War ends, and the Union Pacific begins laying track west.

1869
In April, Central Pacific workers break a record for laying the most amount of track in a single day.

1869
On May 10, the Central Pacific and Union Pacific rail lines are joined at Promontory Summit, Utah.

GLOSSARY

American Civil War: a war fought from 1861 to 1865 in the United States between the Union (the Northern states) and the Confederacy (the Southern states)

avalanche: a large mass of snow sliding down a mountain or over a cliff

ceremony: an event to honor or celebrate something

difficult: hard to do

engineer: someone who plans or oversees the building of something

explosive: a kind of matter or device that produces a powerful blast

immigrant: one who comes to a country to settle there

investor: one who spends money in order to make more money in the future

locomotive: the wheeled machine that produces the power to pull a train

Mormon: a member of a Christian church founded in the United States in 1830

spike: a long, pointed rod often made of metal

stagecoach: a closed, horse-drawn wagon used to carry people and mail

telegraph: a method of communicating using electric signals sent through wires

FOR MORE INFORMATION

Books

Lynette, Rachel. *The Transcontinental Railroad*. New York, NY: PowerKids Press, 2014.

Zuchora-Walske, Christine. *The Transcontinental Railroad*. Minneapolis, MN: Core Library, 2017.

Websites

Driving the Last Spike
www.sfmuseum.org/hist1/rail.html
Read about the men who made the transcontinental railroad possible.

Westward Expansion: First Transcontinental Railroad
www.ducksters.com/history/westward_expansion/first_transcontinental_rail-road.php
Find out more about how this feat was completed.

Publisher's note to educators and parents: Our editors have carefully reviewed these websites to ensure that they are suitable for students. Many websites change frequently, however, and we cannot guarantee that a site's future contents will continue to meet our high standards of quality and educational value. Be advised that students should be closely supervised whenever they access the internet.

INDEX